HOW TO MAKE A MAN WANT YOU

BY ANGELA AZZIEM

Prologue

Do you want a man that will be there for you? Someone who will give you the emotional support you need. Do you want someone you could depend on? Someone who will treat you like his queen. Do you want someone who will marry you? If you do, I have the answer to your problems? Follow these instructions, and you will see an improvement in your love life. You could be headed to the altar sooner than you think!

Rules

Rules

<u>Chapter One</u>

Are you frustrated and emotionally drained? Tire of the same old routine? Fed up with your man? Is he doing what you need him to do? Are you tired of dating? Does your man take you through a lot of drama? Have you been lied to, time after time so he could get you into his bed? Are all the men you date pretty much the same? Do you see yourself feeling a little insecure? Do you feel you are not being taken seriously? Have men hurt you over, and over again for different reasons? Are you tired of trying so hard to be loved? Do you need a man that will be there for you,

Rules

and give you some emotional support? Do you want someone you could depend on? A man that will treat you like a queen and give you your respect all the time. Do you want someone who will remain a friend even if the relationship does not work out? Do you want someone who would go to the lengths of spending money on you to please you? Do you want a man that will ask you to marry him? Do you want a man to protect you from harm's way? Do you want a man that will take you home to meet his mother? Do you want a man to do what you want him to do? Do you want someone who will marry you? If you do, I have the answer to your problems?

THE FIRST RULES OF DATING

First steps when meeting a man worthy of your time, get his phone number. Do not give him yours until you have had a chance to talk to hm a few times to see where his head is. Ask him a few questions like his age. How many children does he have, and does he plan on having more? Ask him how many siblings he has and where he come in as?

This is an important question because, it is not good to clash?

Rules

Check to see where he fits in this category. If you are also the only girl or baby girl in your family, you two could clash when it comes to getting your way. You both could be too immature to cope with each other's ego or one of you will want your way when dealing with each other most of the time when decisions need to be made. Choosing someone with the same sibling position does not turn out to well most times and does not allow you to grow from each other's life experiences. The only time it may work out is if you both were the oldest child of the family. This situation will give you both strengths and maturity to work out problems between yourselves and you both will feel the need to

Rules

want to protect each other. Make sure you ask him about the relationship he has with his mother. The chances are if he is good with his mother, treats her well, and gives her proper respect, then he also may have the ability to do the same with you. The most important question that I find detrimental to every woman is the relationship he has with his father. If a man worships his father there could be some serious issues carried on into your relationship. If his father was not a good person. Ask him what type of father he has, and what is their relationship like with each other. This question will give you a lot of answers to the possibilities of this man's character and who you are trying to get yourself involve with. Most likely if the father was or is a cheater, and was an irresponsible father, then more likely the man you have just met and are talking to will turn out to be the same way or have some remarkably close similarities, because as they say, "the fruit does not fall too far from the tree." If a man tells you that he and his father had or has a wonderful relationship, and his father was or is good to his mother; and is a family man who enjoyed raising him and his family, then you have a good chance of meeting a good man for yourself. These questions must be asked because most of the sons end up like their fathers even when they try not to. When you find out the answers to these basic questions, and you feel comfortable you can go ahead and give the man your phone number. At least the man would know that you are interested in him. Once you have given him your phone number, stop calling him. Give him a chance to call you. I know this may seem hard for you to do if you are anxious to find that special one in a hurry. The reason I said let him call you is that if he calls you after all the questions you had for him shows that he may be interested in getting to know you better, and when a man calls it is because he has been thinking about you. When he calls you for the first time, do not act surprised and anxious. I want you to be calm and pleasant. Make him

Rules

think he at least has a chance with you, but keep the conversation limited. Do not reveal too much about yourself too soon. Limit the conversation to about ten minutes, and then politely tell him that you must go. Makeup anything like I must finish my laundry, or you must prepare dinner, or runs some errands. Tell him anything to make you seem like you are an active person and not someone desperate waiting on his call. Let him know you enjoyed talking to him, and that he could call you back later like tomorrow. This will make him feel curious, and if he is interested in you, which I know he will be, he will call you back. I know from experience that men like to know what is going on in a woman's mind. Believe it or not, a man is very nosey. He wants to know everything he possibly can about you, so he can know how to approach you. He wants to know if you have a man. How many children you have? Are there any chances of getting you into his bed? How can he make you like him? Yes, he will be calling you back trust me. When you get a call back from him act surprised. Smile when you talk to him most people can feel this over the phone. If you give off negative energy, he will feel it. Smiling will give him the impression that you are a pleasant person to talk to and this will put him at ease. Men are more sensitive people when it comes to feelings. Even

Rules

when they act tough as nothing hurts them, they are more sensitive to hurtful words than women. Instead of crying about the things said to them they get mad or distance themselves for a while to heal or some just run for the hills, because you bruised their little ego. When you make him feel at ease, he will be able to open more and reveal a little more about himself to you. Prepare yourself for this question. When was the last time you were intimate? Men always ask this question. This question helps them determine how they will approach you for sex. Take a deep breath do not get angry or excited. Pause for a couple of seconds to make him think that is a touchy subject for you.

Rules

Politely say you are celibate. He is going to say something like wow! Or why are you celibate? How long have you been celibate? I want you to tell him that it has been six months or a year ago since you have had sex. Pick one or the other regardless, if you just had sex yesterday. If it has been years since you have had sex, then just be honest with that. This will either be a challenge for him or a nightmare. You just tell him you are taking a break from your last serious relationship to find yourself, and to give your body a break. Most likely, he will like your self-control and willpower. He will think he has a chance to get you to change your mind about sex. This situation here is when your power comes into play. Men tend to think that they can make a woman change her mind about sex, and her way of thinking and make her see things his way. It is like a game to him a sense of victory, and power when he makes a woman change her mind. Now at the same time, he does not like a weak woman, someone that will give in so easily to him. This will make him seek challenges elsewhere. If a man is interested, he is going to try everything he can to get you to give in to him.

Rules

If you hold off from giving him sex long enough, you will be able to get him to the altar and receive the love and respect you deserve!

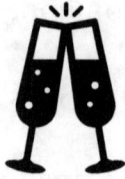

Rules

<u>Chapter Two</u>

When you go out on your first date, make sure it is a public date, and not a private one. It will make him ask for another date. The second date should be public too. Try to keep it simple, like a movie, dancing, dinner, or a concert. This way you can see how he behaves in public. You want to see if he is mean to the servers or if he is picky. The third date can be a private one. A dinner at home if you are feeling comfortable with his vibes, so you can find out where his head is. If you have children do not let him meet them yet.

Rules

Children should not be seen until after you have become comfortable with your man and exclusive. I suggest after three months because you must know what type of man you are dealing with before you introduce him to your kids. Your kids do not need to be exposed to someone you may not want to keep around in your life. Ninety days is plenty of time to tell if you are going to be compatible with him or not. If he asks, when can he meet your children, say "Soon after I get to know you better?" If you are still interested in this man, start complimenting him on his good taste in whatever it may be. If he likes music tell him he has great taste. If he likes sports tell him this makes him sexy. If he likes to cook tell him that this turns you on. This will make him start cooking for you. If he knows he may have a chance to get you into his bed he will do it. A man's objective is to get a woman into his bed. He wants to sleep with you even if he has convinced you that it is not important to him right now. The bed is where his head is. He wants to be able to reveal his nature and his true power, his ability to show you his powerful pleasing skills. He wants to dominate you. This is triumph and victory for him. He will do whatever it takes to get to that level. The more things you get a man to do for you the more he feels he has invested time in you, and you become his investment.

Rules

Do not worry about him leaving you, especially if he has not gotten any sex from you yet. A man will not spend time doing things for you like cutting your grass, cooking your dinner, giving you back massages, watching boring movies with you, or giving or lending you money to have you leave him for another man without getting any sex from you first. Hell no, he will not! He will feel he has invested too much time and energy trying to be a good guy for you to let some other man slip in and take his spot. A man feels if he has invested his time, and money into you he is yours, and therefore you are like a piece of his property now. I am sorry that it sounds bad, but that is how a lot of them think.

Rules

He will not stand by and let some other man come and steal you away from up under his nose without him getting any sex from you first. That situation will hurt his ego if he feels like he has gone through such great lengths to win you over so that he can have you sexually and you give it to someone else. This will mess with his mind and his ego. When the time is right for you, start bringing up the subject of marriage just to see where his head is. Remember if you want this man to marry you, do not give your sex away too soon. Hold out if you can. Never give your sex away before your ninety-day trial period with him. Make him practically beg for it. He will be so turned on by you, and at the same time, he will have respect for you because deep down inside a man likes a self-disciplined woman. He will feel that you only belong to him and that he could trust you to marry him. He will feel that he would not have to worry about you cheating on him. He will also remember how hard it was for him to get sex from you at the beginning. In his mind, he will feel that you must be hard on every guy the same way. This will leave you with a good reputation with him for a long time.

<u>Chapter Three</u>

NO SEX BEFORE NINETY-DAYS,

Do not give in to your man too soon and give him sex before the ninety-day trial period is over. Just because he is looking at other women. If he is looking at other women so what. If he is a cheater or a man that creeps around on you it is his loss, not yours, and he did not get your bedtime goodies from you so no lost on you. Some men feel it is his job to break you down, so that you will become weakened, insecure, and dependent on him, so that he can steal your

Rules

sex from you without a committed relationship; but if you stand your ground and let him look at other women without worrying too much about it, you will find he is not going to let you go anywhere regardless! It is just a scare tactic. If he is a weak man, he is going to stray a little bit just to get sex, but the women he gets sex from will not mean anything to him they will just be booty calls. He will find them easy, but his main object will be you. The one he cannot have so easily. He is still going to want you because, in the back of his head, he still remembers he must conquer you! Men are hunters by nature. Women are prey, little bunnies, cats, lioness, and in some cases dinner. You know what I mean. We are something they must conquer to feel like a man. During your ninety-day trial period with him, do everything you have to do to keep your man except for giving him your sex. Find out what he likes and what he does not like. Make sure you find out what he likes and use it to your full advantage. If he likes certain foods cook them, let him know you care. Plan a romantic evening for two like for example a day at the spa or a candlelight dinner with a light foot massage as dessert. You know become creative. Sit him in between your legs, and just rub his head.

Rules

Men can be like a pack of boys at times. He will love that great feeling. It will remind him of the time he was a young boy and how his mommy use to give him attention and made him feel loved and wanted. Get him to the point of arousal to where he feels he has to have you, but never give him any sex. You must stay in control of the situation, so it does not get out of control.

Chapter Four

Develop Creativity,

You must create memorable moments, and events so that you stay on his mind. Creating good memories in the relationship is what builds the foundation of a union for marriage, not sex. If sex was the answer to getting and keeping a man, then every woman would have her man and be happy. Giving a man a challenge is what keeps him interested in you. Him seeing you not break down and giving him sexual favors so fast and easy is what is exciting and challenging to him. He will remember you for it, and when he finally conquers you sexually, he will feel that you were worth it, and he has finally won you over. A real man feels he must work at proving his worth before he gets his sex from you. This is a great pleasure for him no matter how much he complains or gets upset at you about it. A man will always try to get sex with a woman, but the woman he will consider marrying is the one who stands her ground until she is ready not him. This is the one he feels he need to have. He will not only respect you, but he will also be honored to have you as his woman. He will see that you are different than the rest of the women who have given him sex fast and easy when he wanted it. He will look at them as easy and you as challenging and special. A male's nature

Rules

is to please the female, and if he feels he can please with no effort or fight he becomes bored, and sometimes looks for other challenges to conquer. Like the lion in the jungle, it must conquer and become king. As a lady, you must give him something to look forward to conquering. Keep your king by presenting yourself as a queen.

<u>Chapter Five</u>

Maintain a Little Mystery,

I still believe in some of the old fashion values. Let the man open the doors for you! He likes to do this for his woman. Do not be so easy to give in to his desires. Let him take the time to get to know what your desires are. Be a little mysterious. Let him try to figure out some things about you on his own. A man does not like when you do not leave him anything to figure out about you. I want you to take advantage of this new beginning of the dating stage you have chosen with this man. This is where you will find him at his most vulnerable times. Ask all the questions you need to

Rules

know about him during this time. He does not know where he stands with you right now, so he will feel the need to answer some of your questions and be on his best behavior to make you feel comfortable about him. His goal is to get to that day when you will have him sexually. Take advantage of this time and utilize it to your advantage. The more you make him wait the more desirable you become in his eyes. If you are interested in him, always show it, but do not let him get you to the point of getting you into his bed. He will try his hardest to do it every chance he gets

Rules

because it is his nature. A man respects a woman who makes him wait a while before giving it up to him. He knows that she is not easy. He knows that if it took him a long time to get the sex that it would take just as long for someone else or any other man to get the sex.

Rules

Chapter Five

Questions He Will Ask You,

My sister's let me give you some advice on how to handle

the things that he is going to bring your way!

1. Why are you still single?

   Your response will be, I am selective.

2. Will I have a chance with you?

   You will say, Time will tell.

3. When was the last time you had sex with someone?

   You say, I am celibate now for six months or you could

   say for 1 year, whichever one you choose is up to you.

4. Why are you celibate?

    You say I am giving my body a rest and waiting on the

    right person I feel is worthy of discovering my body.

5. Do you have a problem with sex?

    You say, no I do not have a problem with sex. I think

    it is enjoyable when it is shared with the right person.

Rules

6. Do you have a problem with men?

   You say, no I do not have a problem with men. I think men are interesting.

7. Why haven't you found that special one?

   You say I am selective I do not go for anyone just because they smile at me. I like to see where they are coming from.

Rules

8. What is your type of man?

You say I do not have a particular type if the man has patience and understanding that is my type. This answer will make a man think he at least has a chance at proving to you he can be patient and understanding to your needs. This will give you the upper hand and keep you in control. This will let him know that you call the shots on when it is time to have sex with him. Trust me you can get a man to do a lot for you before you give him sex. Remember, he is willing to do almost anything for you to get some sex from you, because he wants to conquer you, and empower himself, so play your cards wisely!

Rules

Chapter Six

Here are more questions he will ask you.

1. How long will it take before you give me some?

   You say, I do not know to give it some time.

2. What will it take for me to get next to you woman?

   You say, that is up to your determination.

3. Are you a difficult person to get to know?

   You say, no not really, I respond to good conversation.

4. Are you a tease?

You say, no I do not think I am a tease. I do not like to play with people's emotions. (Sound sincere when you tell him this).

5. Will I have the opportunity of meeting your children?

You say, when I feel the time is right for me, I will let you meet them.

Do not let your man meet your children before you get to know the man yourself. I suggest you wait eight to twelve weeks after you have known him yourself before introducing him to your children. This way if things do not

Rules

work out, no one is confused, hurt, or sorry. Some good advice is to get to know your man's parents. See what kind of relationship he has with them when you go over for dinner or socializing. If you see him yelling at his mom a lot or irritated with his father's comments often, you should take precautions! Pay close attention to what is going on between them. A good, kind, and understanding man will be good and kind to his mother. A patient man will take heed to his father's advice. If you find some of these qualities in the man you are dating, give him a chance to make you happy. If on the other side of things, you find

Rules

your man is mean spirited, and moody with no sense of

humor then by all means run for the hills, and do not look

back! Chances are, he is abusive in some way or has some

mental issues going on in his head. A man with a sense of

humor maybe a little more flexible than a man without one.

Being flexible is the key to understanding.

Rules

Here are some more questions he will ask you, be prepared!

1. How many orgasms can you have?

2. Do you have a hard time coming?

3. Are you a hard person to satisfy?

4. Do you like to have sex in the daytime or at night?

5. How do you feel about oral sex?

6. Do you give oral sex?

7. Do you like oral sex given to you?

8. How do you feel about condoms?

These will be some of the questions he will ask you because

he will be thinking about sex all the time even when you are

Rules

not. He would feel in his mind if he asked you some of these questions, it would get you arousal and in the mood. An opportunity to get you in bed. I suggest that you answer these questions with precaution because he is going to use his tricks to try to get you horny, so he can take control and manipulate you into giving him sex. Remember he only gets sex when you are ready to give it to him. If you want him to marry you, I suggest waiting until at least ninety days after meeting him before you give in to him or make him wait until marriage. Give him some things to do for you to prove he is worthy of your love. Make him invest in you to show you he knows that he is in the relationship for the long

Rules

haul! If you want this man to marry you then you must know there are some unusual things you must do. One good way of keeping yourself from sleeping with your man too soon is to pretend in your mind he is married. Just pretend he is a married man, and you would be committing adultery with him if you crossed that line with him. This will keep you more focused. The more you make him wait, you will not believe what things you can make him do for you. He will treat you like his queen because he will not be used to not getting his way. You and I know that not giving him sex will not be easy, but the rewards will surely be worth it. He will respect you for it. Do not be surprised

Rules

if he threatens to leave you. This will be his way of throwing

guilt around. All men do this sort of thing. If you stick to

your ground, I am sure you will not be disappointed in the

outcome.

Chapter Seven

More Questions He Is Going To Ask You

1. Why haven't you given me any sex yet?

   Your answer should be because I am not ready yet.

2. Do you find me attractive at all?

   You say I find you incredibly attractive.

3. Then why won't you sleep with me?

   You say because the timing is not right?

4. What do you mean the timing is not right?

   You say I am trying to get to know you for who you are. I want to know your likes and dislikes. You seem to have a beautiful spirit, and I am trying to connect with it.

5. Don't you think if we slept together, it would connect me and you?

   You say, it may, or it may not. Sleeping with you is one thing and connecting with you is another. Throw a little knowledge at him to let him know that you are intelligent. Let him know you known the difference

Rules

between connecting spiritually and physically. Let him know that a spiritual connection is more like chemistry. It is connecting on a level of consciousness. Where communication is spoken without words or physical contact. It is being in tune with each other's energy. It is knowing what the other one wants before his or her words are spoken. Even if he might be a little irritated, he will appreciate your intelligence. A man will try and say anything imaginable in his mind to get you to see things his way. If you stick to your grounds and follow some of the advice I have here for you, you will be so pleased with the outcome of your relationship.

Chapter Eight

Show Interest,

I am going to let you in on some things you should do when you are dating the man of your dreams. Some of this information I might have spoken about during the first chapter of this book, but now I am going to reinforce some of it again so read carefully this could help you hold on to your soulmate or the man you think you should be with:

1. When he talks to you, look him dead in his face as if you are listening to his every word even if you are

daydreaming about how many people are going to be guest at your wedding.

2. Let him open doors for you. Men do not like it when a woman is too independent. They like to think they are still good for some things.

3. Find out what he likes, and once you find out what he likes, do a little research on it so that you can both have a good conversation about the same subject. A man likes it when he has something he enjoys doing, and the woman he is with has knowledge and interest in the same things. This turns him on!

4. Find out what his favorite dishes are and start cooking them for him at least once a week. He will get used to you making it for him. They say the key to a man's heart is through his stomach.

Rules

Chapter Nine

A Key To A Man's Heart,

A key to a man's heart is keeping him interested in you!

Sometimes you must do some strange things like:

When he calls you sometimes, pretend like you are not at

home. Do not answer the phone. Let him try calling you

a couple of times in that day before you return his call. This

will stir up some mystery and make him a little curious.

Trust me when I say men like to have a reason to feel a little

insecure. It lets them know you are a little bit mysterious.

Rules

Men love a little mystery in a woman. He finds it intriguing. It turns him on and keeps him on his toes with you. In the back of his mind, he is always thinking of the possibilities of you being with another man. It will also test how he feels about you. Try it sometimes. When your man tries to do things to make you jealous act nonchalant about it. Even if you are mad and want to slap him into the middle of next year remain calm. Keeping your cool will make him think that you are not emotionally dependent on him. This will again make him feel insecure keeping your relationship with him mysterious and exciting.

Rules

Chapter Ten

If a man feels that you are too easy, meaning if he can get to you emotionally, and find out what makes you tick, and get you into his bed quickly, he will feel his challenge is over. He will become bored and will move on to the next exciting challenge. The reasons why men cheat on their women are because they become used to them and take them for granted. Most of the time when a woman capture's her man she becomes too relaxed with him and stops trying to maintain some mystery about herself. She becomes routine and loses her flair of excitement. You

Rules

hear about it all the time. A man will say "When I first met my wife, she was so fun and exciting, but now that she has me, she has become so relaxed that she does not keep herself up anymore and she does not care about how I feel. She has gained a lot of weight over the years, and she nags me to death. She is boring to be around." Try to keep a little mystery about yourself sister. Never reveal everything about yourself. Let your man always try to figure something about you on his own. He enjoys doing that!

Rules

I have a few stories to tell you about myself, and my own life experiences. I will start by telling you my story as a young adult. I could not date until my last year of high school. I was always mature for my age, so as a young adult I decided I was ready to get married. I was nineteen years old when I decided that I wanted to settle down and be a wife to someone. I started dating until I found this handsome tall, thin, dark skin, high cheek-boned, beautiful wavy-haired guy. He was so charming that he made me leave this other guy I was dating for him. He and I started dating. I decided that I did not want to be treated the same way the other guys have been treating me in the past, so I

Rules

decided to take another approach. I took control of my situation. I said to myself, If I want this guy to like me, I must do something different than what the other girls might be doing with him. I am sure he was used to getting things his way. I decided to lay down some rules for myself. I thought about the things that I would do for him. I decided that I was not going to have sex with him until he married me. He and I dated for four months, and when I brought up the idea of marriage, he went for it. We were married less than five months using these methods I am sharing with you in this book. He told me he could not keep his eyes off me. He said he wanted me before someone else snatched me up, so we both got married. He was twenty-one and I was nineteen years old. We were both young, but we both knew what we wanted. We stayed married for as long as we could, but unfortunately, we were only together for fifteen years. We share one beautiful daughter from this relationship, and we remain cordial. What I am telling you is not some fairytale story, it is something that happened to me, and he was not the only person who has asked me to marry him. After my divorce, I have been asked three times for my hand in marriage. I was never ready to marry again, but I kept using my same method of withholding sex, and just getting to know the men for who

Rules

they were without letting sex cloud my judgment. I wanted to know their likes and dislikes. I kept them happy in other ways that did not include sex, but once I got to know them, they were not the men they pretended to be, so we went our separate ways. I may have broken a few hearts along the way, but I did not create soul ties that come from having sex with a person and having your soul become dependent on their soul and their soul dependent on yours. You must choose wisely who you have sex with, but that is another story for another time. A man always wants something he cannot have. He will keep trying until he breaks you down, manipulate your mind and steal your precious lovemaking machine that is between your legs.

<u>Chapter Eleven</u>

My First Date,

I have a story I would like to share with you. I will be doing this throughout this entire book, sharing stories with you, so that it may keep you out of trouble. You see I did not have a strong female role model; my mother was an old southern girl. She was seventeen when she married my father, and they stayed together until he passed away. They were married for forty-five years. The one thing she did very well was catered to her man (my dad). I was not allowed to date so she never talked to me about boys or about things men

Rules

could do to hurt me as a woman. She may have known about some things, but I did not know about them, because she never tried to share her experiences with me or protect me from her experiences. I think she did not have many experiences to share because she only was with one man besides my dad. My mom's favorite lines were "A man is going to be a man." Whatever the hell that means. I remember going on my first date. I was about seventeen years old. I met him through a friend. I was so scared, maybe it was because I was from the suburbs, and he was from a big city. I do not know, but whatever it had me scared. I was still a virgin, and he was not.

Rules

He kept on asking me questions about sex. My heart was full of fear. When he asked me why I was still a virgin, I knew he was up to something. I knew then he wanted to have sex with me. I asked myself what did I get myself into? Anxiety took over me. I was sorry that I had chosen to go out on a date by myself with this guy. He was a total jerk! He changed my innocent life forever. He made me think about how bad things can get when you date a person you did not take the time to know. Let me say from experience please take some time to get to know a person. Ask all the questions you need to feel comfortable before you go out with him.

Rules

If you do not feel like dating the guy you just met, tell him.

Do not let him pressure you into going out on a date with

him until you are ready. If he is interested in, you and cares

about your feelings he will wait. He must understand how

you feel. A man who genuinely cares about you is a man

that will wait for as long as it takes.

Chapter Twelve

More Questions He Will Ask,

I have other questions I will share with you. I want you to be well prepared for them when your guy starts to ask you. Here are some more questions he will ask:

1. Do you like foot massages?

   You say, of course, I do. Why you ask? Do you give them all the time?

We all know this is just one of the tricks to soften you up, so it could lead to sex, but just play it cool. Let him give you one if he chooses to but remain calm when he rubs your feet. You should know that if you make the slightest sound of pleasure, he will be turned on by it. It will make him aroused, and he will try to get some sex. When he is giving you the foot massage, please remain calm and moan inside your head not out loud. We all know a foot massage feels good to us, but do not let him know it feels extremely good.

2. When are you going to let me give you a full body massage?

   You say, when the time is right, I will let you know.

3. What is the matter are you scared?

   You say, of course not! Do I have something to be afraid about?

4. Would you give me a foot massage?

You say, sure but you must have nice-looking feet.

When would you like one?

You should know a man's penis hardens when he is being touched or rubbed by a female. It does not matter where you rub him. He just gets sexually aroused. Be incredibly careful! Stay in control this is just one of his tactics. He hopes you get turned on by rubbing on his feet and his body. Remember a man will try anything, and almost everything to get you to sleep with him.

Chapter Thirteen

How Do You Know When A Man Is in Love With You?

When a man is in love with you, he will be the most daring man you have ever met in your life! He will do some strange things. One time I had a friend so in love with me that I had asked him to shave his facial hair, and he said okay. I was young and I did not know any better. I gave him some Nair Hair Remover. I told him that it was what women used to take hair off their legs and it should work well on his face. He said okay and put some on his face. I did not know what would happen if he put that Nair on his face. I told him to do it and he did it, and because he loved me. He tried it. I thought it was the most impressive thing he had ever done for me. I knew he did it from his heart. I was wrong about using the Nair Hair Remover. Oops! It made his face bruise up like blueberries. What did we know we were young and naive? I felt so bad for him afterward. He proved to me he was so in love with me. He completely lost his mind. I did not know he would prove his love that way. Most of the time women know that men can be complete jerks, and sometimes we forget that they fall in love too! When men fall in love, they fall in love

Rules

hard! I believe when a man falls in love, he can be a little dangerous. I say this because a man takes a little longer to fall in love with that person for the rest of his life. I believe when a man falls in love it is because that woman has offered him something different that he feels he cannot get from anyone else. He may become a little protective and a little possessive. Afraid of losing what he feels is good. I have heard some men say that certain women have made their hearts beat to the point they thought their hearts would stop beating and die without that woman. Sometimes we do have men that will kill themselves or their women when they feel the relationship is over because it hurts so badly

Rules

for them and they are not used to feeling that much pain.

Men are less tolerant of pain than women. Pain damage

them more psychologically than physically.

Rules

<u>Chapter Fourteen</u>

Let me tell you a story about something that happened to me a long time ago. I had met this man at an athletic club. We had good conversations, and we enjoyed each other's company. The chemistry was right. We had a lot in common. We both enjoyed the same things, and when we were together, we felt a sense of peace with each other. I had just gotten a divorce six months ago, so you know I was still carrying around some baggage. One evening, we spent a nice quiet time together watching a movie and talking. When the movie was over, you know what he wanted? He wanted sex! He started easing his hands on one of my thighs as he kissed me softly. He started kissing me on my

neck, then my shoulders, and a little nibbling on my ears.
The next thing I know we were in my bedroom on my bed.
He manipulated his way into my bedroom by getting me
aroused and confused! I did not remember him carrying
me into his bedroom. The next thing you know I was in
my bedroom. The forbidden area. I never let men into my
bedroom unless I know I want them there, and it would not
be to lie down and fall asleep. Do you understand what I
mean? Okay getting back to my story. He started taking
his clothes off at this time. I felt turned off! I knew I did
not want to be doing that. My mind was trying to think of
all kinds of ways to get rid of him. I came up with some

excuse by crying. The cry got him to back off me. He asked me what was wrong. "I know you are still hurting from the break-up of your marriage," he said. I just nodded my head in agreement. "Yes, you are right," I said. There was nothing wrong with me. I just needed him to back off! And put his clothes back on. When I saw the little penis he was working with, I was turned off automatically. It gave me something to cry about. I made up a lie and told him that I did not think that I would be ready for sex again for a while. I never called him back again. Do you know I seen this fool out in some nightclub! He had the nerve to come over to my table and say that he still thinks about me and that he still wants me. He said we had some unfinished business to handle. He asked me what I thought about him, and about getting married. I am telling you when you use the rules in this book on a guy, make sure it is a man you could consider being with. If not, you could attract the wrong type of guy that you would probably have a hard time getting rid of. Every time I run into this guy, he always asked me to call him. He just does not get it! I do not want to be bothered by him. Have you ever wondered why the guys you do not like or the ones you are not interested in always seem to be the ones madly in love with you? If you do not have the answer to this question, I am here to tell you it is,

Rules

because you have become a challenge to him or them. A man likes tough love regardless of how much he might complain about his woman being a little rough or bossy to him. A man does not like a wimpy woman. It can turn him off! I know because I have a lot of male friends. Most of my friends are males, and this is what they tell me themselves. My male friends tell me they do not understand why women give their power away to men. They say it is not what a real man wants. They also said a weak wimpy type of guy likes to take a woman's power away because he feels threaten and insecure himself. My male friends say that a real man would let a woman be who she is, and not change her essence of what made him attracted to her in the first place. I am telling you from experience, and from just talking to my male friends. You must be challenging to a man for him to fall in love with you. Stop being so boring and routine. Test your man out from time to time. When you say you are going to call him, sometimes do not call him. Watch the response you get from him when he calls you back. He is going to wonder and try to figure out what is going on. He is going to have insecurities about his place in your life. This will keep him from being too cocky and sure of himself. I have gotten many more things from men I consider my friends than I

Rules

have ever gotten from men I decided to sleep with too soon!

Be careful when you choose the man you consider worth

your time to be with when you use the rules of this book. If

you do not want him, tell him, and let him go. If you like

this guy, and you are planning on using this book to help

you keep him, make sure you are going to stick around and

not play him. This book is not used to hurt anyone on

purpose, be careful. He will be hurt after he follows all rules

you have given him from this book, and you still leave him.

If you do not want to be with him, he will never forget you,

and maybe he will probably never forgive you for leaving

such a good impression on his mind and his heart. You will

be a hard act to follow. A man can get sex. It is quite easy

out here. Women are throwing themselves at men. A man

is not going to marry you because you give him sex. He is

going to marry you because you touch his heart.

Chapter Fifteen

In His Bed Too Soon!

I would like to share my story from a few years ago. I was dating this guy who I met at a club. He was fine as wine and very sexy to me. It was love at first sight, so I gave him eye contact. He looked at me and smiled. I was so overwhelmed with joy, and I became kind of nervous. I walked away from his viewing area. I knew that he knew that I was interested in him. Before the night was over, I went over to him and gave him my phone number. I think he thought I was desperate for him because he did not call me for a month. When he did call, I messed up by sounding, so excited and out of control like a schoolgirl. I started talking too much! I was giving him too much information about myself too soon. I was happy he decided to call me. He could feel the excitement in my voice. He knew from that day on he could take the control from me, and call all the shots, so he did. He controlled the day we had sex, which was on our second date. I do not regret that day we had sex, because it was wonderful. I just regret the day I turned over my power to him. He knew I was weak for him. I spoke earlier in my book about not giving a man too much information about yourself too soon.

Rules

A man will take what he knows about you and use it against you. Going back to my story. The guy I was seeing knew he had me where he wanted me. He figured it out, I was falling in love with him. He knew he was a great catch because it turned out he was a manager for a big automotive company. He had a degree in International Public Relations where he traveled from time to time. The public loved him. He was a people person, and I forgot to mention he had a gorgeous body. He was solid muscles. He looked strong like a football player. I messed up and gave him some too soon! Even if he had a lot going for himself, I should have given him something challenging to work for.   He was used to getting his way with women because he did have a lot going for himself and beautiful dimples when he smiled. I was really into this man. I let him dictate the relationship. He told me when he could come over, or when he could make love to me. I was being very stupid. He never took my feelings for him seriously. He probably thought I was another stupid woman giving him what he wanted. I was stupid because I thought he was my man for a year. I found out later by a friend of his that he was in love with this other lady, who he had been chasing for about a year. She did not like him his friend said she would not give him any time of day. I heard she was a stripper paying her way through school, and he did not

Rules

impress her. She was popular with the guys like he was with the ladies. I saw her at the gym a few times. She is as pretty as I, but because he could not have her, she was the one he wanted. He liked me but he did not love me. I saw the love he had in his eyes for her. He was loaded with confidence, but when he saw her at the gym, he was like a shy boy. I could not believe it. I was not insecure when he was around her, because I knew and could sense she did not like him. It showed in her face. To her, he was just a paying customer. He was too stupid to know I was in love with him, but it was my fault for not having rules for him to follow. He took me for granted.

Rules

I ran into him several years later he was still single. He told me when we were together, he was a sex addict. He was trying to tell me in his own way that it was not all my fault. I know from my own experiences, and from talking to my male friends about what a man wants, and what he does not want. Do not think because you give your man sex it will make him fall in love with you? If you think this way you are setting yourself up for heartbreak.

<u>Chapter Sixteen</u>

There is this club where I use to attend for ballroom dancing. I started going there a year after my divorce because it relaxed me, and it was good cardio exercise. You may know how it feels if you have ever been divorced. If you are divorced, you know it feels good to break free your first couple of years and let loose! You want to be out and about to find out what you have been missing out on. I started going to this club where there would ballroom dance. It is where I would go to relax and observe people,

Rules

and their personalities and behaviors. I have seen many
things go in that club. I have seen many married men go
up in there to see if they could take a woman home. I would
see cheating couples in the parking lot sitting in cars making
out with someone else. I have seen unhappy married
women come up in there to see if they can go home with a
lonely guy. In this club you see many different situations
without trying to spy. I just came to dance and drink my
cranberry juice. People these days just make it obvious
what their motives are. I have seen this one situation where
this guy was trying to talk to this lady. He started off asking
her to dance. He was a good dancer too. I could tell she

Rules

had low self-esteem by the way she held her head. You could see the nervousness on her face. I think he knew she was nervous and had low self-esteem. That following week he started showing her how to ballroom a little better. As the weeks went by, I say two weeks later, you could see them growing a little closer. Not to the point where she gave him sex. You could tell she had not given him any sex. I could tell by the way he was all into her. He looked at her as if she were prey, and a piece of meat. He was looking like a wolf in clothing. He was behaving a little possessive as she stepped out to the lady's room. I would hear him say hurry back every time she stepped out. I would hear her say okay. I could tell she has already given him power. This couple stood out to me more than the other people that were in the club. I guess it was because I saw them when they first met and hooked up together, and because I am sentimental when it comes to good relationships and love. I wanted to see how their relationship would turn out, so I kept an eye on the two. By the third week, I saw him come in by himself and stand by the wall looking for women like he used to do. I was looking around for that woman he was dancing with for the past two weeks to come in sometime that night and dance with him. It never happened. He was flirting with other ladies as though he was on the prowl

Rules

again. I thought to myself what a dog he is! I did not see

that lady come into the club anymore for two months.

When she did show up, she did not look the same as she

used to. She kind of looked unhappy. I saw the same guy

she was dancing with two months ago pass her by as if she

were trash, as he tried to hit upon another lady. I have seen

her watch his every move as he tried to push up on another

lady. I have watched her watch his every move as he tried

to charm other women. I felt kind of sorry for her, but then

I thought to myself she must have given up her power and

had sex with that man.

Rules

I knew she must have slept with her, so he was done with her completely. He got what he came for. I think she might have slept with him too soon! If she would have taken her time with him, and let him play by her rules, he would have still been there to dance with her and treat her like a lady. When you choose someone to love, choose him wisely. Men will always try to see what you will let them get away with!

Chapter Seventeen

Other Questions He Will Ask You

1. How old were you where you when you started having sex?

   I advise you to answer this question at your own risk but remember he might use it against you later.

2. When are you going to let me make love to you?

   You say, when I feel you love me.

3. Am I wasting my time with you?

   You say, I do not know. Do you feel that you are wasting your time with me?

4. Will you ever make love to me?

   You say, sure when I feel you love me, and I love you back.

5. Do you think I am going to suffer forever?

   You say, why do you feel you are suffering? Sex is not something I owe you. It is something that is given out of love and trust, and I want to make sure I can trust you.

6. Why are you taking your problems out on me?

   You say, why do you think I am doing that? I am taking my time with you because I do enjoy your company. I do not want to mess things up.

7. Do I make you happy?

You say, of course, you do. That is why I am taking

my time with you because I do enjoy your company.

I do not want to mess things up between us.

This answer will kind of calm him down for a couple of

days. I say a couple of days because he is going to go home

to think about it and see if you are worth his time.   When

the time comes, and he feels that you may not be worth his

time, he is going to think about letting you go, and the

consequences that may come with it. This will build up

anxiety for him. He will be thinking of another man getting

Rules

ahold of you as soon as he breaks up with you, and the possibility of you given in to that other man. He is not having that, so he will weigh his pros and cons. He will weigh up his options and stick around. Do you want to know why? I will explain why. He is not about to take several months of begging and taking you out to dinner and spending money on you to let you get away and have that on his mind. He sees you as his investment now, and something special. It steams a man up! I cannot say all men are like this, but most men feel that when they have invested money, and quality time into you they think that you belong to them. They do not want to think about

Rules

another man coming in on their territory. This will almost destroy him and his ego. Therefore, when you hear something happening like this you always hear of two men fighting or killing each other. A situation of something like this will make a man strike out in anger to claim what he feels is his. He will never want to see another man move in on his territory. On what he thinks is his property.

Chapter Eighteen

The Different Types Of Men,

We are going to talk about the different types of men women are dealing with in today's world. It is getting extremely tough to find a good loyal and faithful man. I know they are out there somewhere. You do have men in this world who are looking for good faithful and loyal women as well. Loyalty and faithfulness do not belong to one gender. It is a conscious decision made by each individual.

Rules

The Mama's Boy

Let us start with the mama's boy. I have a couple of friends who are mama boys. They are difficult to deal with sometimes. They can be complicated men and make your life a living hell because they demand a lot of attention, and most of them are high maintenance as well. There is a lot of immaturities that come with him. If you find yourself falling in love with this type of guy you must be prepared to do a lot of cooking for him, and your cooking has got to measure off to his mother's cooking. He is going to test you at the beginning of the relationship to see if you even like cooking. He starts by throwing you a little hint like "Why don't you throw something on the grill." Of course, this will

not bother you at first. You might think it was cute of him

to ask you this. Once you do this for him the first time with

no problem, he is going to ask you again very soon at some

point. He has no problem with demands, and he is very

manipulative too. He will start asking you to cook a little

something for him every time he feels he can. He will

become comfortable with the idea of asking you a lot. You

will find yourself not going out as much to eat. Most

mama's boys like to bring their women around their

mothers, so get used to spending a lot of time with his

Rules

family. He will expect you to love his mother as much as he does. You are never to criticize his mother's cooking or anything she does because he will see it as a personal attack. He feels she could not do anything wrong in his eyes. Mama's boys tend to find women with similar characteristics as their mothers. Someone who will baby them and attend to their needs. Mama's boys are high maintenance and do not like getting their hands dirty. You usually find that these men are unable to withstand the pressure of life. A lot of these men have trouble making a good hard earn living in life. They usually take the easy way out in life. It is usually hard for them to adjust to change and a lot of them are reckless with other people's money and their own too. They like to nag you about how life is not treating them fairly, and a lot of them carry a lot of excuses and give reasons why they cannot make things work out right for them. Most of the time they have a hard time making their own decisions and you will find them calling up their mothers for just about everything. There was a guy who I was dating who happened to be a mama's boy. Every time we spent time together, I would see him dialing his mother on his cell phone. The next thing you know he would tell her everything we were doing. I kid you not!

Rules

One day he and I had just finished having sex, and he was on the phone calling his mother. I think he had a serious problem. I had to get rid of him. He was laid off from his job, so he made every excuse in the world as to why he could not get up in the morning to look for a job. He lost his car and his job and most of the time he would be over to a relative's house playing Play Station. Can you believe this guy? A thirty-three-year-old man, playing Play Station 2 for many hours of the day. Instead of looking for a job. I got rid of him, after I figured out, he was a loser and did not want anything out of life. He knew his mother would bail him out of everything and believe she did!

The Baby Boy

The next type of man we have is the baby boy. I do not know which ones are the worst the mama's boys or the baby boys. Well, I do know this, the baby boy of the family seems to want everything his way. He wants to control the relationship. I know this type very well because I was married to this type. He always wanted things to go his way. I remember cooking him his first meal prepared by me. I was so excited I decided to go home from work just a little earlier than usual, so I could prepare this meal. It was our first apartment we shared, and we were newlyweds. We

Rules

were only married for a few months. I went home to fix this

wonderful salmon croquet. It is when you turn salmon into

salmon patties by adding eggs and batter and deep-fry them

in hot grease. They taste so good! I also made a side of

butter beans, and rice along with cornbread. I was so happy

that day. I have always been a romantic at heart, so I was

happy to do this for my man. I had prepared for our meal

to be eaten by candlelight. When he walked in the door

about an hour later, he said yum! It smells so good to in

here what are you cooking? "Why don't you wash your

Rules

hands and come find out," I said. I asked him to have a

seat. I served him his plate and then I grabbed mines and

sat across the table from him. The first thing that came out

of his mouth before he took a bite was "how many eggs did

you use"? He asked. "Why," I asked. "You are supposed

to use two eggs as mama does," he said. "I am not going to

eat this," he said. "It still tastes good try one," I said. "No,

my mother uses two eggs I am not going to try that," he said.

He had a very nasty attitude. This was our very first real

fight as husband and wife. He did not want to take a chance

at trying my dish to make me happy, because it was not the

Rules

way his mother made it. I knew from that day I was dealing

with trouble. Believe me, more trouble came

behind that. He wanted me to wait on him hand and foot.

I was only nineteen I had to cook dinner for him every day.

He did not like leftovers or to eat out of paper plates,

because he said his mother did not raise him that way. He

never washed any dishes, but he sure knew how to create a

lot of dishes by eating so much. His ways made me so

angry inside that I became resentful of him. What I did for

him was never good enough for him. I suggest you make

sure you can deal with the baby boy of the family.

Rules

They come with a lot of immaturity, and complaints. If you
are okay with it, go for it!

Rules

The Insecure Type

Let me introduce you to the insecure man. This man can make you paranoid and almost lose your mind, because of his insecurities. An insecure man can make a woman feel ugly, causing a lot of damage to her self-esteem. This type of dude is known for the type who does a lot of stalking. He is the kind of man that calls you several times a day. He is the type of man I call the bug a boo! Why? Because he will bug the hell out of you. In the beginning, he will shower you with his love, and you will think it is cute until you become smothered. He does not know how to go home.

Rules

He will make you feel guilty for sending him home. He is
the type that would like to be around you all day and all
night. When you are not around him, he will try to accuse
you of being with another man. This guy will try to make
you feel insecure about your self-image. He will say little
things like you look a little heavier. Did you gain weight? I
see some grey hairs popping up. Why did you use that
shade of lipstick? When you two are out together, he will
make sure no other guy can get a glimpse of you. He will
be the one all in your face blocking your view of other men.
If you are looking at something or someone his eyes will

Rules

zoom over to the viewing area too. He will ask you what you are looking at or do you like what you see? When you tell him, you are going to the restroom, he might say let me walk out with you. I must go too. The insecure guy can be a thorn in the ass. Let us talk about the one I had. He was so insecure it was frightening. He ripped the toenail off my big toe trying to get to my phone to see who was calling me through my caller ID. He did not mean to, but his paranoid jealousy made him space out. A friend of mines happens to be on that call. He was a male friend, and someone I met way before I started dating this guy. All I remembered

Rules

was, he ran over my big toe with my computer chair trying to brush me over to get to my phone before I could. He ripped the toenail right off my foot. I bled badly which made him pick me up and carry me into the bathroom to run water on it to it stop bleeding. He wrapped it up with a ban aide too. I could tell he felt bad that it happened because he looked so terrified. He said he just was not thinking straight when he saw another man's name come across my caller ID. We went to the movies after he cleaned me up. He carried me to my seat and pretty much carried me throughout that day. I ended up staying with him for a while because he had some good qualities about himself too. Another time he became

Rules

insecure, was when my brother called me and left a message on my phone. I went to go check my messages and he said he wanted to hear. I said sure I had nothing to hide. I let him hear who called me that day. I was trying to put his mind at ease even though I did not have to. When he heard my brother's voice message, he went crazy! Me and my brother are remarkably close, so we call each other baby. I think of my little brother as my baby, because he is the only boy in the family. When this man heard my brother say "hey baby" he started shaking and went outside to smoke a cigarette. He then asked me to call my brother back to see if it was my brother, so I did. I asked my brother to speak to him to calm him down. My brother asked why? I explained it and my

brother and I both thought it was funny. My brother is cool,

so he spoke to him and explained it was the way we talked to

each other. This insecure man did go on to say he apologizes

for acting like a fool. He tried to change the subject and

make me laugh by making a joke and picking fun at how bad

his behavior was. He was very humorous. I forgave him

because he could laugh and make you laugh at his mistakes.

He was talented at making me laugh. I think he could have

been a comedian if he were not so jealous and insecure, but

the longer we dated the worst he became. His behavior got

ugly. It was the last straw for me when he made up a story to

Rules

make me feel bad. He said it was a man in the restaurant who told him I always hung out there to pick up men and take them home for sex. May I remind you this was our favorite restaurant, we enjoyed eating there at least once every week. It is where we first met. I was there because I needed to eat after studying so hard for an exam. He kept staring at me and smiling as if he knew me, so as I was leaving the restaurant, I asked him if I knew him from somewhere. He said no but he has seen me eat here lots of times. I was impressed he noticed and never approached me before. He asked me for my number I told him, no, but I would take his. I called him two weeks after that because I had to focus

Rules

on my exam, and that is how he and I began dating. Now getting back to this insecure man's lie. He said it was some guy in the restaurant he and I hung with who told him that he better watch himself because I go there to pick up men and take them home for sex. I was mad as hell. He made it sound so believable that I was willing to drive up to the restaurant to confront the guy for being such a liar. I tried to convince him it was a lie. He told me he believed the guy. I ask him why? He said for some reason he does believe him because I always have guys smiling or saying hello to me when we are together. I asked him, why would I of all places go to our favorite restaurant to do something like that; when

Rules

I know how jealous and insecure you are? If I was going to do something like that, why choose your favorite restaurant? He took me through mental distress trying to convince him it was all a lie. It went on for five weeks. He then confessed it was a joke, and he wanted to see if it was true. At this point, I thought he was a monster and broke up with him. The sex was great with him, but his mind was messed up! I had to run for the hills!

The Midlife Crisis Type

This type of man has a serious problem going on in his mind. During his midlife crisis, he thinks life is passing him by. He thinks he is losing his cool, or manhood, and his sex appeal or something. He acts foolishly! This type of guy likes to run around in Jerseys and T-shirts with a baseball cap on his head because he lost all his hair. You will find his type hanging around strip clubs, and casinos. This type of guy chases after younger women in hopes of keeping his youth. You will find this type of guy dressed like a teenager, and saying things like, what's up? He tries to keep up with

Rules

the latest fashions of the young guys. Knowing his big belly does not look good in those tight shirts anymore. He does things you would never think a grown-ass man would do like drag racing or clubbing with a lot of women. It is like he has lost his mind. He is also insecure about his age. He does not like looking back at his past and is very secretive about his past. He really would hate it if you guessed his age. The midlife man has roaming eyes. Every young woman looks like his dessert. They look at every young girl in a skirt or tight pants they can get some attention from.

Rules

They like to test themselves to see if they still have the game because they feel they need to. Most of these men eventually make a fool of themselves and cause the woman they are seeing to lose interest in them quickly. They try too hard to be young and cool. When this is a turn-off for most women. Most women like a mature man and someone comfortable with who he is. Being comfortable in his skin makes him sexy. There is nothing wrong with a man growing old. If he keeps himself in good physical shape, he will always be able to have a younger or older woman.

The Control Freak

This type of man is the worst kind of all in my opinion. This man has a serious problem that can sometimes lead to a woman's death. If you have one of these in your life or plan on dating someone who is controlling be careful. This kind of man hates to see you happy. He feels he must control everything in your life. This type of man can drive a woman into a mental institution or depression, and sometimes to her death. Beware of his temperament! If you are wearing lipstick that you know is very sexy, and hot and he tells you to take it off because it makes you look like

Rules

a slut or a whore this is usually a warning of more problems

coming later. If you two have dinner plans for two, and you

decided you want to look very sexy for him, and you put on

a dress that is hot, but not sleazy or slutty, and he still makes

a negative comment like "What are you trying to do attract

another man? This is a sign of jealousy and control.

Control freaks will try to destroy every bone of confidence

you have in you. I dated this one guy who was a control

freak. He tried to control the type of lipstick color I wore.

He tried to control what I brought. How I paid my bills.

How I shopped for dinner, shopped for close, how I

enjoyed my life, and how I took care of my house. He was

mentally disturbed. These types of men are usually temperamental. You will see their moods change many times during the day. This is the type of man that usually asks you a lot of questions, especially during the beginning of your relationship. He will be the one asking you questions. "I called you the other day. Why have you not returned my phone call?" He will also ask. "Where were you the other day? I came by, and you were not home." Here is a real warning if you are dating a control freak. "If I ever catch you with another man, I will beat your ass!" Joking or not joking leave him as soon as possible. Chances are he is serious. Here is another one. "I am addicted to you. I do not think I could ever let you go. I love you to death." This may sound good at first but trust me it is not cute at all. Especially not with a control freak. This type of man wants your whole life to revolve around him. He will eventually tell you how to talk, walk, look, and what type of friends you should have around. He will make you spend less time with your family. He will want you all to himself. I advise you not to ever get too serious with a control freak. Let him know upfront that you do not want anything serious with him because if you do not, he will make your life miserable. Control freaks are hard to get rid of.

The Wimpy Type

This type of guy is weak for you, and he will practically do anything for you. If you ever had this type of man in your life, you would know what it feels like to have real power in a relationship. This man will be at your beck and call. People say that wimps do not have a backbone, because he does everything his woman tells him to. Is this all bad? Now wait a minute, there is a difference between doing things for someone you love because it makes you happy, versus doing things for the person you love because they told you to do it; and it makes you feel bad and abuse your emotions. These types of men can be such a turn-off.

Rules

I know I prefer to have a man with a balanced mind. I do not always want him to tell me yes. If I am wrong for asking, he may get mad, but I will respect him for it. I can say out of all the guys I have mentioned to you I have not yet dated a wimp guy so I cannot share anything with you based on my experience. What I can say is if you are a strong woman, dating a wimp will eventually become a turn-off for you because there will be no challenges in the relationship and without challenges, there is no growth. Believe me, you will become restless with him and start looking for a man that can give you a healthy challenge. Think long and hard before falling in love with this type. I would not want to see you cheating on him.

The Player Type

This type of man is the most hated of the group. He thinks

he is God's gift to women. He will lie his ass off to get what

he wants from you. I have a story to share with you about

this type of guy. I have dated this kind of man before, and

it was like being in a nightmare because everything he had

said to become a part of my life was a lie. When I found

out the truth about him, I thought he was insane or should

I use mentally ill. One day I was invited to a birthday party

by a friend. He happens to be a male friend of mines, and

we did business together, so I went. It was at a dance club.

I was enjoying myself and socializing with everyone. I was

then introduced to a nice-looking guy, by the birthday man.
We both introduced ourselves and shook hands. I was
sitting at a table full of empty chairs. I asked him to join me
since he was just standing there with a drink in his hand.
He started a conversation with me asking me how did I
know the birthday boy? I told him, and from there on we
started talking. He asked what I did for a living. I told him
I was an author. He asked me what book did I write? I
told him it is called "The Weight Loss Bible." He and I
got on the subject about food. We had a healthy debate
about foods that were bad for you. This is when he became
interesting to me. I like that he was able to challenge me.

Rules

After our challenging conversation, I asked him if he knew how to dance. He said yes, I do. We both headed to the dance floor. The DJ was playing one of my favorite songs. He took me by the hand and pulled me in closer to him so he could slow dance with me. He held me in his arms. It was comfortable. I felt protected. He was so smooth and light on his feet. When the song was over, we went back to our table. I remember asking him was he married because this felt too good to be true. He said, "No don't even worry about that, because I have been divorced for a year and a half already." He went into details about what had happened between him and his ex-wife that made them end the marriage. I was like wow! His ex-wife sounded like my ex-husband. It was like we were reading from a chapter of my marriage life experience. We hit it off quite well that we forgot we were there to celebrate our friend's birthday party. We stayed in each other's company that whole night talking and dancing. When it was time to leave, he had asked me for my phone number, and a chance to get to know me better. I took a couple of seconds to think about it before I responded. I said yes, it was okay to have my number. I figured since we both shared the same friend that he could not be that bad, so I gave him my number. He said he wanted to walk me to my car, so, I let him. After he walked

Rules

me to my car, he went over to his car. It seemed hilarious we both were driving the same type of vehicle. We both looked at each other and laughed. "I do not believe this," I said. "He said, I don't believe this either." We knew from this encounter we would stay in contact with each other, and we did. He called me two days later. He told me our mutual friend had told him I was having some work done on my basement. I told him yes, I am. I asked if I had already gotten three estimates. I told him no not yet, but I have gotten two so far. He said great because he would like to be the third estimate. He said he does home repairs and home improvements, and he knew he could beat anyone's

Rules

price. I allowed him to look at my house and give me an estimate. It turns out he had given me the best price of three bids. He was a thousand dollars cheaper than the other two companies, so I let him do the work. Everything was going great for the last four weeks. We were having great phone conversations. We had a lot in common. He seemed like such a nice guy. We went on our first date after five weeks of talking. He took me on our first date to a spa to rub my feet and massage my back. After we left the spa, we went out for dinner. He pulled my chairs out for me to sit. As we were getting ready to eat dinner, he received a strange phone call. I said it was a strange phone call because

Rules

he excused himself and took the call and headed for the
bathroom. He told me he would be right back. I did not
think anything of it, because I know when people own their
own business, they sometimes must take calls throughout
the day. Especially a construction business. It can get all
kinds of strange calls during the day or night, so I started
eating what was on my plate. It took him about fifteen
minutes to return from the bathroom. His eyes were red
when he came back to the table. It looked like he was
distressed, so I asked him what was wrong? "It is my sister,"
he said. I said your sister. "Yes, she is having trouble with
her husband. He keeps putting his hands on her, so she
wants me to come to get her, and bring her to my house,"

he said. I said wow! We better leave and go get her. He said he told his sister that he was on a date and once his date is over, he would gladly go get her. He said he was tired of his sister taking him through the same drama. I comfort him by holding his hand and letting him know that if there was anything, I could do to help let me know. After we left the restaurant, we went over to his best friend's house. I guess he wanted to show me off to his friend. He introduced me to his best male friend and his female friend. We had a good conversation. They thought I was pretty and had invited me to come over again for dinner, and drinks with them. We left his friend's house and he drove me home. I had a wonderful night. I say it was a good first date. He was a very romantic guy. It was like a dream come true for me because I always wanted someone generous and romantic the way he was. He catered to me, and he was very attentive. He made sure he called me every day. Even when he was at work, he would call me. You could hear men in the background working when he called. He would take me back to the spa to rub me down whenever I had asked him. That spa was cozy and romantic. He rented it out by the hour, so it would be only me and him there. My birthday was approaching soon, so we had planned to go to a concert that day and just enjoy ourselves. A few days

Rules

before my birthday, he had told me his dad suffered a stroke, and he and his family had to rush his father to the hospital. I was blown away by sadness and grief for him and his family. He told me that he and his dad were not on good speaking terms since he was thirteen. He said his father was too strict on him and made him go live with his grandmother until he became a grown man. To make a long story short. He said he was feeling guilty about his dad because he and his father did not get along well. I was feeling bad about how he was feeling about his dad's stroke. It looked like he was having a hard time dealing with the situation. He would spend all night at the hospital comforting his mother, so he said. When I would ask him

if he wanted me to come down and sit with him, he would

say no it was okay. He said the hospital would not let me

in the intensive care unit. He said that he felt that his mom

would not be in the mood for meeting me at this time, but

as soon as this crisis was over, he would make sure she knew

who I was to him. I understood his situation, so I did not

pressure him about it anymore. Two days had gone by and

his father was doing much better. He told me his father was

even joking again. He said his father was still in danger, but

he was handling things very well. Every night he would go

to the hospital to comfort his mom. He said he and

Rules

his dad made peace with each other. He said his father told him to look after his mother. On the day of my birthday, he and I had plans to go to a concert to see some of my favorite bands play. I was so excited that day because I was going to a concert with someone I was falling for. He was such a romantic hunk of a guy. He said he had something planned after the concert. I waited for his call that day because he always called me around a certain time just to say hello or good morning. Well, he did call me that morning, but it was not to say good morning. It was to say that his father slipped into a coma, and it was a possibility that he was not going to be able to take me out for my

Rules

birthday. I felt so bad that I told him not to worry about my

birthday I would be fine. He said he would still try to take

me to the concert for my birthday since I had already

bought the tickets. He said give him some time to be with

his family, and he would play it by ear and let me know

something before the concert started. He said he needed

to be there for his mother. He said she was becoming very

hysterical and tearing up the house looking for insurance

papers. He said his dad always took care of his mother very

well, and that she would not know what to do in the event

of him passing away. He said his mom is clueless. The

time became near to the starting time of the concert. He

Rules

told me to go ahead without him because he still wanted me to enjoy myself on my birthday, so I hurried up and called a friend to join me at the concert. She made it just in time before the concert started. She asked what happened to my male friend. I explained that his father had slipped into a coma, and his mother was not taking it well. We both felt bad about the whole thing. He said he would keep me posted on any changes. I felt so bad that I could not enjoy my birthday. I felt guilty for having a good time while someone else had a bad time. I did not enjoy myself that night. Me and my friend had left for home before the concert ended. I felt worried, but there was nothing I could

Rules

do. When I got home there was a message on my
answering machine. It was him. He was letting me know
that he was sorry for not being there for my birthday and
that he will make it up to me. He told me to have a good
night and he would talk to me in the morning. He called
me the next morning and asked me who did I end up taking
to the concert. I felt that was a little strange being the first
question out of his mouth, but I told him anyway. He then
asked me if I enjoyed myself. I told him I could not enjoy
myself. He said he was sorry for ruining my birthday. He
said he would make it up to me.

Rules

Three days after my birthday he called me with bad news to say his dad passed away. He said his mother ordered the plug to be pulled on his father because his dad did not want to be seen in a comatose situation. He said his father was a strong man. He told me he was so stressed and if he did not do something about it, he was going to be the next person dead. He asked me to go away with him. He said he needed some quality time with me before he planned his father's funeral. He was desperate for time alone. He asked me to see if I could get time off to be with him. He said please he needed me. I explained to my boss what had happened, and I needed time off. She gave it to me with

Rules

no problem. She knew I was a caring type of person. He called me to see if I was able to get the time off. I told him yes. He said okay great. He told me to pack my bags. He said he was going to finish the job he started on that morning, so he could be all caught up. He said he would call me as soon as he was finished so that we could leave. A few hours passed. I decided to give him a call to see how far along he was on his project. He said he was almost done and to give him forty-five more minutes, and he would call me back. An hour had gone by and I have not heard back from him. I just thought maybe he was running a little behind on time, so I called him, and got no answer.

Rules

Fifteen minutes after I called him, a woman called me. She asked me if I was trying to reach that number. I told her I apologize I must have dialed the wrong number. She asked me what number I was trying to reach. I read her the phone number. She said it was the right number. She said her name was Sonya she was his wife. I was confused, I said no you are not. He is not married. I was thinking she was just baby mama drama. She explained to me he had been with her all day. She seemed genuinely nice, so I started to listen to her talk. She said he has been at the house with her all day putting up a fence for their backyard. I asked her was she playing with me. She said no. As Sonya and I were

Rules

talking, I could hear a man talking in the background. She asked me if I heard him talking. I told her I barely heard anything. She said she was going to ask him something, and she wanted me to hear his response. She asked him where his phone was. I did hear him say he must have dropped it. She asked me if that was his voice. I told her yes that was his voice. She told me that he was her husband and they have been married for seven years. I explained to her that I did not know that because he had told me another story. I then gave her my name and began asking questions about him. I asked her if he just recently lost his wallet. She said no they just went on vacation. I asked her about his father's death. She said his father was not dead. She said

that he and his father do not get along they do not talk to

each other. I asked her about his sister moving in with him.

She asked me what sister moving in with him? She said it

was a lie. Sonya said she must have been the sister he was

talking about because she was planning on leaving him for

good. She said he had cheated on her before, but he has

begged her to come back home to stay with him. I told her

he had planned a weekend for us to be together. She said

he did huh! I asked her to put him on the phone. She gave

him the phone. He did not know who was on the other end

of it. He said hello. I asked, are you married? He

Rules

recognized my voice. He sounded like he had just had the wind knocked out of him. He said yes, I am married. I asked him why did he do that to me? He said he did not know why he felt twisted. His wife told him to say how he felt about her. He told me he was in love with his wife, and that he was going to stay with her. At this time, I thought I was experiencing "The Twilight Zone." I went into shock. My body became numb. I started laughing in disbelief. I told him he ruined my birthday because I was worried about him and his father. I reminded him, about asking me to take time off work to be with him, and how he could have endangered my life with his wife. All I heard him say was,

Rules

I am sorry! I hung up the phone and started to cry. I felt like I was being punished for something I must have done in the past but was not aware of. I felt depressed, humiliated in front of my friends, family, and my boss. I felt disgusted and betrayed all at the same time by the hands of this player. He did not care about who he hurt. His wife was eight months pregnant. She apologized for her husband's behavior. She said she knew it was all his fault. In his mind, it was all about him. Pleasing himself and playing a game. This is the reason I chose to share my story with you. There are some sick and twisted guys out there waiting to prey and take their problems out on innocent

Rules

women.   In my opinion, the player type is the most dangerous of them all.   He is like the devil who knows how to get you to win his trust, and then he goes into your heart and attacks it.   He knows how to tap into your emotions and bring you joy.   He also knows how to bring that joy to an end and leave you with a broken heart.   In his mind, he thinks he is doing you a great service.   He is deceiving, destructive, and possessed with a calculating spirit like a devil.   In his mind, he thinks he is God's gift to women.

Chapter Nineteen

Being A Different Kind of Woman

I am now going to talk about ways you can behave that makes you different than any other type of woman. Why? Because different is what a man likes. He does not like you doing the same things as other women in his life. He wants you to be something special in his eyes. A man likes to feel he has captured a diamond in the ruff. In a man's mind, his woman is his trophy piece his accomplishment. Starting today I want you to behave as if you are a superstar. I want

Rules

you to think that you are a star. You do not have to be pretty or rich to feel this way. I want you to tell yourself you are a superstar a diamond every time you are in the company of a man. Eventually, your mind will align with your thoughts, and help you develop a new personality. I am giving you information on what I know works. It was something I tried doing a few years ago. I had gotten more than what I had bargained for thinking I was a superstar. I have attracted some popular celebrities, business owners and local celebrities thinking I am a superstar. I dated two singers in the same year. I felt great every time I told myself I was a superstar. Every time I think I am a superstar, and tell myself I am a superstar; I can feel an energy inside of me. A tingling sensation that felt positive and electrifying. It gave me chills. My spirit became enriched with the energy of superiority. It made me feel as though I was someone special. I had men I never dreamed would look at me or beautifully see me. Every time I told myself I was a superstar it made me feel beautiful. It was like an internal magnet. My male friends who I knew for many years started looking at me in a different light. Some of them have started to develop feelings for me. I was attracting guys like a magnet. "I am a superstar" are the words you should tell yourself every day before you walk out your door. It

Rules

should be the words you say softly to yourself when you are in the company of a man. What is the old saying? "So as a man thinks, so shall he become." Think like a superstar and watch you get your confidence back. Men like it when a woman has enough confidence in herself to know what she likes and dislikes. He will even respect you for it. Always walk with your head held high and try to keep a smile on your face. Never let anyone break your spirit.

Chapter Twenty

Rules You Need To Have For Yourself

1. Do not be too emotional. Learn not to react to everything you are feeling.

2. Do not talk to any of your female friends about your new man.

3. Only love those who love you back.

4. No sex before your ninety-day trial period.

5. Do not date married men.

6. Do not live with a man before marriage.

Rules

7. Do not reveal yourself to men too soon.

8. Give a man a chance to prove how much he

loves you.

9. Take your time when dating.

10. Do not settle for any man.

11. Be honest with yourself.

12. Do not try to change a man.

13. Do not confess your love to a man first, before he confesses his love to you.

14. Do not let him meet your children before ninety days.

15. Do not call him until he calls you.

16. Do not overwhelm him with your problems.

17. Do not be so dramatic.

18. Do not be so accessible.

19. Do not say yes to everything he offers you.

20. Remind yourself you are the superstar.

Rules

Do not make it easy for him!

The worst thing a woman can do in life is make life too easy for a man. A man is not designed to have his life made easy. They love a challenge that is why they play sports, go to war, and even cheat on women that are good to them. A man once told me that. When a man asks you out on a date, do not make it easy for him. Let him pick the place, find out when you are available, and provide transportation to get you there. Okay, maybe drive your vehicle. Do not go Dutch on the first date. This will make you seem desperate. He will either judge you as being too independent, or as being lonely, and in desperate need to be with someone.

Rules

Remember this is a man you are dealing with. How you start with him, he will expect you to keep it up. So do not go Dutch when you know deep down inside you want him to pay for the date. This is the time you should be yourself. First impressions last the longest in a person's mind. Be pleasant, but at the same time be honest with him and yourself. If he does not open doors or pulls your seat out for you, just tell him you are used to having these done for you and you see it as being polite. Maybe he only does these things for women who request it, or he is afraid of taking your independence from you. In any case, let him

Rules

know how it feels it bothers you. Do not let him keep you out longer than three hours on your first date. First dates should be kept short and simple. This is where you are trying to get to know a little about each other to see if you have anything in common. If he tries to keep you out longer than three hours on the first date, tell him you must end the date now, because you have something to do. If he wants to see you again, he will make another date with you. Remember it must be on your terms. Do not let him make a date for you. If he calls you on Thursday to make a date for Friday, tell him you cannot, because you already have plans. Let him know that you must at least have a two-day notice. This will let him know that you are not desperate, and he must respect your time before he just makes plans. He will gain respect for you because he will know that you are not the kind of woman who sits around and wait for him. You are a busy woman with options. He will start thinking to himself, wow! She is going to be a challenge she is not going to let me come in and out of her life as I want it. What I mentioned before, men love this. He likes a woman who knows what she wants and gives him her rules to follow. I know this because I have a lot of male friends

Rules

who confessed this out of their mouths. Women have so much power, but we do not know how to use it. I always hear men say, "If I had a vagina, I would never starve. Women have it so easy, but they do not know how to use it to their advantage."

Withholding from Sexual Activities

What you can accomplish by withholding all sexual activities. Let me explain what you can accomplish. I was looking back at my life experience and discovered that when I did not give my sex away, I got a man to do things for me willingly. I have been asked to marry four times. I have had someone pay for my car insurance for a year and help me get a new car because he did not want to see me struggle with my older vehicle. He said he thought I was such a cool person to be around, and he appreciated me as his friend. I had someone do some home improvements

Rules

to my home because he said he wanted to see me and my

child happy. I have had someone who would take me out

to eat with him all the time just to have a good conversation,

and he would pay for everything even when I offered. I

have had someone pay my house note when I could not

because he thought I was such a good person to be around.

Me looking back on these experiences make me say, Wow!

I did not have to take my clothes off to get the attention or

the help I needed when I was down. These men found me

desirable, because of me and not what I had between my

legs. I was just being myself. All I did was laid down some

rules from the beginning of the relationship with these guys

Rules

and stuck to them. I let all of them know that I did not want to have sex with them. I made sure that I kept things on a friendship basis, and if things became uncomfortable or out of control with our friendship, I would always let them know that I could not continue being friends with them anymore if they could not respect me not wanting sex. I notice the more I withheld from having sex with men I dated, the more they felt the need to do things for me. I would strongly suggest withholding sex from the guy you are dating to see how far he would go to get it. Sex is his goal; he loves to count the days when you will let him get it. If he knows he can get it easy with no effort, he will get it and be off running to the next woman looking for a challenge. Ask

yourself this, during the times you did have sex with a man

too soon, did he stick around long enough to fall in love

with you? Did he call you the next day? Did he make

excuses as to why he cannot? Did he respect you

afterward? Did he become distant? Did he go out of his

way to do special things for you? If you could only answer

yes to two of these questions, I suggest you think again

before jumping into someone's bed too soon. If you are

not challenging enough for him, I guarantee you he will not

stick around for the long haul. Now, if for some reason he

does stick around, I know he will not be content with you.

Rules

He will have wondering eyes. Why? Because you were not

a challenge you were too easy. Deep inside his mind, he is

wondering if you sleep with or slept with many other men

as easily as you did with him.

How To Tell If He Is Not Into You

If you have ever been in love before you know what it feels like to love someone. You wake up in the morning with nothing, but him on your mind. You go to work and daydream of the last conversation you had with him. You get excited thinking about the plans you have with him coming that weekend. You think of ways to make him happy, and you go to bed with him on your mind. I am here to say, if a man is into you, he will be thinking and having the same feeling as you do. If a man is into you, you

Rules

will not have to sit near a phone waiting on his call. He will

call you several times a day. At least twice a day. If he is

not into you, he will call you maybe every three days to see

how you are doing, just so he can make sure he stays on

your mind, and to keep you emotionally tied to him for a

booty call. If a man is into you, you will not have to ask him

for a date, especially at the beginning of the relationship.

He will make the first move, and planned the date, because

he wants to get to know you better. If a man is into you, he

will ask you what you like and dislike. He will try to make

Rules

sure he remembers, and you will hardly have to say what is

on your mind. When he is into you, he will try to figure out

ways to keep you happy. When he is into you, there will be

no guessing about his intentions. He will make them clear.

How To Hold On To Your Guy

Remain cool throughout the whole time you spend in your relationship. Never let him see you worry too much about his whereabouts. If he says honey, I am going out with the boys tonight. I want you to say okay that is nice have a great time and be careful. If he missed your calls a couple of times do not sweat or freak out. Men do that to test us sometimes. Keep a level head do not let your man think you are trying to control his whereabouts. Every man needs his space, no matter how much he is in love with you. A man must have some quality time to himself so that he can

Rules

process things in his mind. Whenever you tell a man something, he thinks about what you said. He may never tell you this, but he does. A man is a thinker by nature. He thinks more with his mind than his emotions. Sometimes when you cloud his mind with emotions, he needs to have time alone to process them, and sort things out. This is absolutely the truth about them. Have you ever heard of the old wise tale? "Don't tell a man too much, because he cannot handle it." There is some truth to those words. A man processes everything you tell him. Even

Rules

when you think he is not listening to you he is. He may not

respond to everything you present to him at that moment.

A man needs time to think about things. He does not like

to be made a fool, so he feels that he needs the time to soak

in what you have expressed to him, and weigh things out in

his own time, so he could know how to deal with it, and

you.

Exposing Too Much Information About

Yourself

If you tell a man too much about yourself, you could be setting yourself up for rejection. When a man becomes angry with a woman, he uses everything she told him about herself against her. He will use it against you, and this is a guarantee! Be careful with the information you share with your man. Some things are better off left unsaid. Especially if you want to keep some mystery about yourself. Most of the time men are interested in your past, so they can see how to approach you. In some cases, it is okay to tell a man a little about your past. Especially if you were abused by your ex-lover, but in most situations, it is not good to talk about your past hurts. It is good to talk about the positive things you went through with your ex-lovers if they want to know about it.

<u>Chapter Twenty-One</u>

Stop chasing him,

Another thing I have learned about a man, and that is if you act like you are not interested in him, it makes him try even harder to impress you. The chase is on! I would like to share with you something that happened to me many years ago. I was seeing this man who I thought was so gorgeous. He was tall, dark, and very handsome. He made my heart skip a beat every time I saw him. He knew he had that kind

Rules

of effect on me. I think it kind of tickled him to know the

effect he had on me. Every time he would ask me over, I

would jump at the chance. It did not matter what I was

doing, or what I may have had planned for that for myself.

He would call and I would get all excited. All he would

have to say is "Can you come over," and like a fool, I would

drive to his house. I was hooked every time. I would say

sure, I will be right over. I have given my powers to this

man. Let me share with you how he felt about me. He said

he just wanted to be friends with me because he was still in

love with his ex-wife, but at the same time, he was sending

Rules

me mixed messages. Every time I went over to his house,

he would always try to see if he could have sex with me. I

adore him, so of course, I would let him get me aroused

until I could not take it anymore. I would tell him no! and

to stop! When we got to the point of having sex. He could

not understand why I would tell him no and stop. I would

tell him to stop because I did not want him to make a fool

out of me. He told me exactly how he felt about me as a

friend, so I gave him his respect. I would always throw our

friendship up in his face when he got to the point of wanting

to have sex with me. This would make him remember what

he said to me about being friends. During that time, I had met another nice man and a good guy. He was all about taking care of business. He treated me with respect and he never pressured me for sex. This was not his mission. He simply wanted someone he could rely on. A partner he could make money with and enjoy life. This was my type of guy. He made me feel at ease, and when he took me out, I knew we were going to have a good time. I enjoyed his company. He always gave me something to think about whenever our date ended. He was intelligent, and he was something I had not come across in a long time. He had this mystery about him. It was not a weird mystery or

Rules

something bad. I sensed a mystery of something missing in his life, and this is what kept me excited about him. Do not think I am weird because I like mystery. He did tell me about the things I needed to know about him, but I could feel a sense of loneliness about him. You would not know it if you knew him, but I am the type of person who pays attention. Now getting back to the story I am trying to share with you. I started dating him. I felt I could become not only a good life partner for him but also a great business partner with him too. I stopped calling the dark, tall, and handsome guy because I knew he said he just wanted to be friends. I was now enjoying myself with the new mystery man. He and I have been going out on dates and enjoying each other's company. We have been seeing each other for about three months. I get a call from my friend the tall dark and handsome guy. He asked me what have I been doing? I told him I have been enjoying life. Guess what? Now he wants me to spend more time with him. He asked me what I was doing to occupy my time. I told him I found a wonderful guy who was interested in me. It made him aware that other men are interested in me too. It then changed his mind about me. He started calling me more often and asking me to spend some quality time with him. He stopped asking me to come over for sex. He started

Rules

asking me out to spend quality time with him since I told

him I was not interested in a relationship with him anymore.

He could not understand why I changed my mind about

him. I explained to him that I understood how he still feels

about his ex-wife and that I hope that he and she would get

back together. I guess this made him realize I have moved

on. He asked me why was I giving up on him? I told him

I did not like to compete with other women. I told him I

was happier with my new friend because he was honest with

me and has not asked for sex. This made him think about

what he did to me. You should have seen the look on his

face when I gave up on the possibility of us ever being together. It seemed as if he knew his game was over. He started asking me why I want him and his ex-wife back together; and that maybe he and I might be together in the future. I told him that I did not want him in that way anymore. I just wanted to be friends, and now I can say he seems like he cares about me. He calls to see if I am okay. He calls to see if I could go dancing with him. I must say I cannot believe I am only friends with that tall dark and gorgeous man. I had a chance to choose him, but I chose not. I have learned to be patient and I listen to what a man

Rules

is trying to make known. If you get caught up in a man's looks and do not pay attention to his game, he can break your heart at the end. Reframe from lending out your sex before you see where his heart is. I must say since I have been a little more patient with choosing the best guy for me. It has saved me a lot of dignity and I have self-respect. I guarantee if you stick to my rules on how to make a man love you, you will save yourself a lot of heartaches. You can have the man of your dreams now if you start following the rules. Do not think because you give a man sex this will make him stay and love you. If you believe it will, you are going to continue to be hurt like most single women. A real man does not only focus on sex. He wants to see what other qualities you have to offer. Every man wishes he could find a good faithful loyal wife. He wants to know if he will be able to rely on you for moral support. He wants to know if you will be there for him even if he happens to fall on hard times. If you only have sex to offer him, he is not going to be truly loyal to you. He is going to see who else is out there that can supply his other needs. A man can get sex anytime anywhere. It is quite easy to get sex these days.

Rules

A Woman Is A Precious Gift From God

As a woman, you must learn how to respect yourself a little more. In the old days, our mothers would say "girl to keep a man happy you must be a great cook or know how to make good love to him." In today's world there is a little more you need to do to get a man to fall in love with you. You must pay attention to what he is trying to make known. You must offer more than sex because sex is easy to get in today's world. The internet, cell phone, and social network

Rules

sites. If sex is the answer to love, we would all be married

and in love. Be patient with yourself. Allow yourself some

time to get to know the guy. Always consider yourself a gift

from God. A man can only do to you what you allow him

to do. Behind every great man is a great woman keeping

him together. The reality is a woman is a man's weakness,

but she also makes him strong.

Rules

Being That Beautiful Woman God

Intended You To Be

Always be beautiful. Meaning never degrade yourself or lower your standards to please a man. Remember you are a superstar. Stay strong and stand your ground. If a man makes you feel uncomfortable and pushes you into doing something you are not comfortable with, think about it. Ask yourself if he is worth it and what are the benefits you are getting from it? Is it worth it? Will the outcome make you

Rules

happy? If your answer is no, do not do it. In the end, you will not feel good about yourself. Did you know that every time you have sex with someone, a part of yourself is left with them and a part of them is left with you? Would you like a part of yourself to be left inside a player? As a woman, you must choose your partners wisely, and carefully. Stay beautiful, meaning do not let someone persuade you into doing something out of character you

Rules

would not normally do. Learn to be a little more patient, and make decisions with your mind, and not with your heart. Most of the time a woman's heart gets her into a lot of trouble. Always respect and stay true to yourself. Learn to develop your higher level of consciousness from here is where you can see more clearly.

<u>Tips For Looking And Feeling Good</u>

On the first date wear colors like red, which increases sexual desire, and activity, or white for balance and harmony, and protection against negativity, or black for breaking free from bad habits, and brings or opens self-confidence. One of these colors is good for a first date. They are memorable colors, and he will not forget your first date either. Keep your skin glowing by using cream to cleanse your face instead of soap. Soap dries the skin. Buy cleansers you can

Rules

use that will not dry your skin. Cold creams, or plain hot water, and even Noxzema keeps the skin glowing. Another good product to use is Witch Hazel it is a mild cleanser, and many people of today only think it is used for cuts and bruises. It is a mild cleanser, and you never have to use soap. You can just wash your face with hot water and take a cotton ball, wet it with Witch Hazel, and watch your skin glow each week. You can also use cucumber juice to tighten your skin. Slice the cucumbers in pieces and use as needed.

Rules

I recommend putting it on just before going to bed to tighten your skin and smooth out wrinkles. Petroleum jelly works well too. It preserves the skin and keeps your face baby soft. I suggest using it at night before going to bed. Dab some under your eyes too. It is also good for removing make-up and it smooths out wrinkles the longer you use it. Remember to brush your teeth twice a day. Soak your feet at least once a week and put petroleum jelly on them. In the wintertime, you can put petroleum jelly on your feet at

Rules

night, and put socks on, and sleep. It will absorb into your feet to make the heel and the soles of your feet soft in the morning. Men love women who keep their feet in good condition it makes you look nice in a pair of open-toe shoes.

Rules

You Are The Superstar

Remember you are a superstar! "God's precious Gift" stays sweet, and always remain a lady. Stick to the rules of this book, and watch you shine! You should see some positive changes coming your way soon. Remember behind every good man should be a good woman. You are that half that makes a man whole. Stay positive and you will get that man you want.

Rules

<u>Acknowledgments</u>

I want to give special thanks to my beautiful daughter Sadia for being so supportive of my writing, and to my family Julie, Vivian, Ali, and Toni and friends, and to all my readers. I will continue to write about certain topics and give you the quickest way of solving some of your daily problems with my quick guidebooks. Do not forget to check out my other books. "The Weight Loss Bible," "Silent Evil," "Dating Rules For Teenage Girls," "My Dog Benji." "Jack The Bumblebee And Friends," and "Lulu The Cat."

Rules

Thank you for your support, and may God Bless!

Angele Azziem

Rules

Rules

Rules

www.ingramcontent.com/pod-product-compliance
Lightning Source LLC
Chambersburg PA
CBHW060256290526
45789CB00001B/333